W9-BMU-590

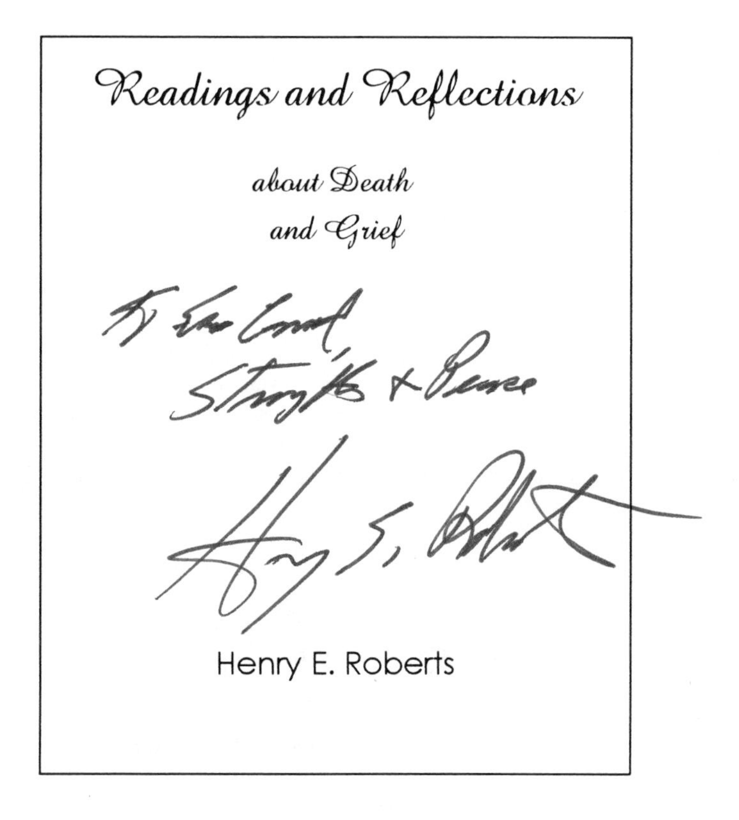

Ardara House, Publishers
Pensacola • Florida

Library of Congress Control Number 00-134450

ISBN 1-888676-08-6

This book may be ordered by mail from the author.
But try your bookstore first!

Dr. Henry Roberts
First United Methodist Church
6 East Wright Street
Pensacola, Florida 32501
850 432 1434
Hroberts@PensacolaFirstChurch.com

This book is dedicated
to the memory of
my brother,
James Thomas Roberts
September 29, 1939 - October 14, 1998

He taught me how to run,
how not to be afraid,
and how to shoot a basketball.
He taught me how to love my family.
He taught me how to let other people go first.
He taught me how to meet a stranger
as an old friend.
In the last year of his life,
he taught me how to deal with death
and die with dignity.

❦

Thomas Merton in his book, *LOVE AND LIVING,* writes descriptively as if he had known my brother:

. . . it is important that the end of life itself should finally set the seal upon the giving and the sacrifice which has marked mature and productive living. Thus man physically and mentally declines, having given everything that he had to life, to others, to his love, to his family, and to his world. He is spent or exhausted, not in the sense that he is merely burned out and gutted by the accumulation of money and power, but because he has given himself totally in love. There is nothing left now for him to give. It is now that in a final act he surrenders his life itself. This is "the end of life," not in the sense of a termination, but in the sense of a *culminating gift,* the last free perfect act of love, which is at once surrender and acceptance: the surrender of his being into the hands of God, who made it, and the acceptance of the death which in its details and circumstances is perhaps very significantly in continuity with all the acts and incidents of life — its good and its bad, its sins and its love, its conquests and its defeats.

❦

Table of Contents

Introduction — 9

Part One: On Death — 11

Part Two: On Grief Work — 31

Part Three: On Re-Connecting — 65

Part Four: On Serenity — 79

Part Five: On Hope — 85

Part Six: On Other Loss — 115

Introduction

There is about our lives a blending of joy and sadness, light and darkness, hope and despair. When the time of laughter is over and there are empty chairs at the family table, because we have lost through death the ones we love, there is great suffering and deep hurt. We don't love deeply without great pain.

Within the short period of eighteen months I was brought face to face with the truth of death through the loss of my father at the age of eighty-six and the death of my brother at the age of fifty-nine. Death is real and my grief, even at this writing, is hard to deal with. It is compounded by my feelings as I lose friends within my congregational family and attempt to minister to those who grieve.

Out of my own pain I have assembled material and have written of my awareness of finitude, love and hope. Perhaps this work will better equip me and others to be what Henry Nouwen has called *The Wounded Healer.* His concept is that the person who has suffered injury or loss, including death, is often more fully capable of entering into the grief of another. My hope is that the sharing of my experience will encourage and help others in pain seeking to deal creatively with the harshness of reality. Death and other grievous losses are an inescapable part of being alive, but we can deal with them and not be destroyed by them. Also, as a matter of fact, realizing the harshness of death often enables us to cherish the good days of closeness and laughter.

In this selection of readings and reflections I have included material from a broad range of sources which illustrate different attitudes and understandings about death. I have not attempted to say that there is only one understanding of or attitude toward death or other losses which reflect the absolute "correct" position, theological or otherwise. I only have sought to affirm that there is a way to move through the darkness and pain of one's losses.

With God, there is always hope.

Henry Roberts
Pensacola, Florida
July, 2000

Part One:

On Death

It was helpful to me when I made peace with the meaning of Elisabeth Kubler-Ross's statement that "We can only truly live and enjoy and appreciate life if we realize at all times that we are finite."

I could have so easily lost my life on a fateful morning when I was struck by a car while jogging. During the two years of recovery I came to see life, and especially my life in a human family and in Christ, as a precious, sacred gift. Against the threat of the dark void of death, life in its unique beauty became visible.

It is not in running from death as "the grim reaper" that we will find peace, but it is in facing finiteness and being embraced by one who is not our enemy but ultimately our friend. Death would not have been given to God's children unless it had a place in His divine plan. Ted Menten writes, "I believe that death is a friend, a fabulous dancer who will twirl me away in my last waltz."

However . . .

the further I am removed from my near-death experience, the more the old temptations to control life and claim false securities of all kinds begin to rule and dominate my days and cloud my judgment. It is helpful to remember that death's clear message is of our finiteness, which stands over us all the days of our life as a sign to remember that we are not of this earth but are merely on a journey with friends through it. Making peace with death achieves the life task of our desire for unity, which ultimately overcomes our fear of death.

Most of our days come and go and we are not confronted by our finiteness , but only when we are face to face with death do we realize what God has given us in our human pulsebeat. Thomas Mann observed this truth when he said, "Without death there would scarcely have been poets on earth." So death becomes appreciated rather than dreaded if it enables us to see more clearly the beauty of life in which we are privileged to live.

❦

The death of those we love
is an inescapable part of being alive,
but the good news is that
we can deal with it
and not be destroyed by it.

❦

Psychiatrist Elisabeth Kubler-Ross is now world-famous for her studies with persons who are dying and with those who have experienced the death of a loved one. Reporter Joe Schoenmann wrote the following account of the psychiatrist's appearance in Las Vegas in 1999.

> Dr. Elisabeth Kubler-Ross, renowned for her work on death and dying, twice choked up in recounting her life's story on Sunday, but left no doubt with the 1,000 people who traveled from across the country to hear her.
>
> She's had a terrific life but can't wait to die. "I can barely wait to take off," the 73-year-old said at Artemus Ham Concert Hall on the University of Nevada, Las Vegas campus.
>
> Kubler-Ross flew from Scottsdale, Arizona, to Las Vegas as the guest lecturer for the Bigelow Chair of Consciousness Studies. Having suffered from numerous strokes, she was brought on stage in a wheelchair.
>
> To a rapt audience, the Swiss-born psychiatrist and author doled out humor in the form of honesty as she told how and why she got involved in the study of death. Her first encounter with death came when she was confined with an unknown illness in a Swiss hospital. In the same "glass cage" with her was another girl. The little girl knew she was about to die, but she welcomed it.

"She was super-duper happy and excited to die," Kubler-Ross said.

In adulthood at the University of Colorado, Kubler-Ross' career took off when she invited a dying 16-year-old girl to talk to medical school students about her experience. At the time, no one was willing to talk about death, said Kubler-Ross.

But since then, and after talking to hundreds of people dealing with their own process of dying, Kubler-Ross said she found many commonalities. Foremost, she said, is the desire by those who are dying to talk.

"There was never, ever one single patient who did not want to volunteer information about dying," she said. "I have talked to 2- 3- and 4-year-olds who talked about it as though it's the most normal thing in the world."

In 1969, she published *On Death and Dying,* which today is standard reading at most major medical schools and graduate schools of psychiatry and theology. In the book she outlined what she called five stages of death: denial, anger, bargaining, depression and acceptance.

"I knew this was my mission, that this was my work," she said.

She went on to write more than a dozen books,

including *On Life After Death* and *Aids: The Ultimate Challenge.*

The audience seemed to revel in her reassuring words, especially the insights she gave on her many years of talking to those who were dying.

"Nobody at the moment of death is petrified of it," she said. "It's like taking a tight old shoe off. Taking it off lets the foot become comfortable again."

Kubler-Ross choked up when someone asked her to recount her most exceptional memory. She told the story of a poor woman destined to die because she was "too poor, too everything" to get a kidney transplant. Kubler-Ross decided to give the news to the woman herself. But when she walked into the woman's hospital room, the woman grabbed Kubler-Ross' hand and comforted her, instead.

"Dr. Ross," she said, "if they will not accept me in this garden, God will accept me in his garden."

Monday, October 25, 1999
Copyright © Las Vegas Review-Journal

When I was on a trip to central Florida, I noticed that Kubler-Ross was speaking that very night at a local university. The large auditorium was crowded with over 4,000 people. In her early seventies at the time, she was assisted to the stage. For over an hour and a half she kept every one of us spellbound. She described her research, thousands of interviews over many years with individuals who had experienced death's approach and yet were able to describe their experience. She spoke of many common experiences which grew out of her interviews.

The most comforting of her observations was that "Although many individuals die lonely, there is the common testimony of the presence of individuals with them. We never die alone," she said. The testimony of thousands of interviewees was that at the moment of impending death there came to them individuals, some who had died previously and others who were but distant friends, to assist in the journey beyond the river of life into the next life.

❦

There is no death!
The stars go down
To rise upon some other shore,
And bright in heaven's jeweled crown
They shine for evermore.

John Luckey McCreery

❦

I was much involved in pondering the ideas of life and death, spring and winter, Good Friday and Easter, and the whole reawakening of the world that happens every spring.

One evening we entertained a friend for supper, and he, too, had been pondering such themes, and even shared a work by T.S. Eliot in which there was a phrase something like "in our end is our beginning." That was virtually the catalyst for the form of the text of "Hymn of Promise" which I wrote the next day or two.

Soon after writing "Hymn of Promise" my husband Ronald became ill with what turned out to be a terminal malignancy. As the end neared he asked me to use "Hymn of Promise" as one of the anthems at his funeral service – which was done – and I subsequently (at publication) dedicated the piece to him.

Natalie Sleeth, 1986

In the bulb there is a flower;
in the seed, an apple tree;
in cocoons, a hidden promise:
butterflies will soon be free!
In the cold and snow of winter
there's a spring that waits to be,
unrevealed until its season,
something God alone can see.

There's a song in every silence,
seeking word and melody;
there's a dawn in every darkness,
bringing hope to you and me.
From the past will come the future;
what it holds, a mystery,
unrevealed until its season,
something God alone can see.

In our end is our beginning;
in our time, infinity;
in our doubt there is believing;
in our life, eternity.
In our death, a resurrection;
at the last, a victory,
unrevealed until its season,
something God alone can see.

Natalie Sleeth

John Donne has written:

Nunc lento sonitu dicunt, morieris.

Now this bell tolling softly for another, says to me,
Thou must die.

> Any man's death diminishes me,
> because I am involved in mankind,
> and therefore never send to know
> for whom the bell tolls; it tolls for
> thee.

❦

Sooner or later, and probably more soon than late, you and I must deal with this basic reality about our life: we will die and so also will those we love. We all have to face death! Death is a reality for us all. No one is exempt. It is the most certain of all certainties. This fact must be faced with candor, courage and faith.

❦

As someone pointed out to me recently, the percentage of those who die to those who are born is still 100% – always has been and always will be – one to one. For, as Donne wrote also:

> And what is so intricate,
> so entangling as death?
> Who ever got out of a winding sheet?

❦

People often say, "It was God's will," with the intention of consoling the bereaved. The net result, however, is to cause anger at God for taking away the loved one. To be sure, anger is a normal part of the grieving process, but the blame — the target of the anger — is misdirected.

I have heard this said at a child's funeral. I became so angry I had to leave the room before I spoke intemperately myself. God does *not* will children to die capriciously. He does not have a huge cruise liner for which he must make up a passenger list for people of all ages. God takes no delight in tragic practical jokes. Usually, when this sentiment is expressed, it goes something like, "God just needed some beautiful flowers for his garden, so he plucked little Johnny for his bouquet." Grief is a time when people need all the support they can get from friends, family and God himself. To assert that "It was God's will" that someone died is to cut off the possibility of divine support during the most crucial period of bereavement.

Roger F. Miller

❦

O God, our help in ages past,
our hope for years to come,
our shelter from the stormy blast,
and our eternal home!

Before the hills in order stood,
or earth received her frame,
from everlasting Thou art God;
to endless years the same.

A thousand ages in Thy sight
are like an evening gone,
short as the watch that ends the night
before the rising sun.

O God, our help in ages past,
our hope for years to come;
be thou our guide while life shall last,
and our eternal home.

Isaac Watts, 1719
Psalm 90

Divorce almost always involves the death of a relationship.

In the *United Methodist Book of Worship* is a prayer to be used in a *Ministry With Persons Going Through Divorce*:

God of infinite love and understanding,
pour out your healing Spirit upon [name],
as [he/she] reflects upon the failure of [his/her] marriage and makes a new beginning.

Where there is hurt or bitterness,
grant healing of memories
and the ability to put behind
the things that are past.

Where feelings of despair or worthlessness flood in,
nurture the spirit of hope and confidence
that by your grace
tomorrow can be better than yesterday.

Where [he/she] looks within and discovers faults
that have contributed to the destruction of the marriage and have hurt other people,
grant forgiveness for what is past
and growth in all that makes for new life.

Heal the children [name(s)], and help us minister your healing to them.

We pray for other family and friends,

for the healing of their hurts
and the acceptance of new realities.

All this we ask in the name of the One
who sets us free from slavery to the past
and makes all things new,
even Jesus Christ our Savior. Amen.

United Methodist Book of Worship

❦

Oh, what a poignant prayer is this, prayed finally when the hopes and dreams of a marriage are down the drain and only the dregs of a relationship remain. It is certainly a time for grieving.

❦

Who will separate us from the love of Christ?
Will hardship,
or distress,
or persecution,
or famine,
or nakedness,
or peril,
or sword?
No, in all these things we are
more than conquerors
through him who loved us.
For I am convinced that neither
death,
nor life,
nor angels,
nor rulers,
nor things present,
nor things to come,
nor powers,
nor height,
nor depth,
nor anything else in all creation,
will be able to separate us from the love of God
in Christ Jesus our Lord.

Romans 8:35, 37-39
New Revised Standard Version

Akner, Lois F. Page 47. *How to Survive the Loss of a Parent.* New York: William Morrow, Inc., 1993.
Confronting loss and getting on with your life.

Bayley, John. Page 115. *Elegy For Iris.* New York: St. Martin Press, 1998.

Cutter, Fred. Page 33. *Coming to Terms with Death.* Chicago: Nelson-Hall, 1974.
Confronts the taboos, fears, and anxieties surrounding the realities of death.

Edelman, Hope. Page 61. *Motherless Daughters,* The Legacy of Loss. New York: Dell Publishing, 1994.
A wealth of anecdotal evidence, supplemented with psychological research about bereavement.

Eggen, Julie S, LCSW. Pages 44, 90. *A Gentle Goodbye.* Pensacola, Florida: Sacred Heart Hospital, 1984; Baptist Health Care, 1993.
For parents who have experienced loss of their baby through miscarriage, stillbirth or infant death.

Hammarskjold, Dag. Pages 28, 71. *Markings.* New York: Ballantine Books, 1964. Translated by W. H. Auden.
An intensely personal book concerning the author's feelings about himself and God.

Hayes, Helen. Page 66. *A Gathering of Hope.* Philadelphia: Fortress Press, 1992.
A very personal statement about the religious faith of a famous personality.

Kubler-Ross, Elisabeth. Pages 11, 14, 30. *On Death And Dying.* New York: MacMillan, 1967; *Living With Death and Dying,* 1981.

Lewis, C.S. Pages 38, 39. *A Grief Observed.* New York: The Seabury Press, Inc., 1961.
One of the most moving books about the personal toll of grief.

McCain, John. Page 102. *Faith of My Fathers.* New York: Random House, Inc., 1999.

Menten, Ted. Pages 11, 93. *After Goodbye.* Philadelphia: Running Press Book Publishers, 1994.
Stories that will help you find ways to move forward with honesty and grace.

Merton, Thomas. Page 6. *Love and Living.* Orlando, Florida: Harcourt Brace Jovanovich, Publishers, 1985.
The famous monk writes with unique insight about life, loving, and the values which make life worthwhile.

Miller, Roger F. Pages 22, 34, 48. *What Can I Say?* How to Talk to People in Grief. St. Louis: CBP Press, 1987.
Some basic rules for speaking to a friend in grief.

Miller, Sue. Page 25, *While I Was Gone,* "Daniel's Sermon on All Saints Day." New York: Alfred A. Knopf, 1999.

Mitchell, Kenneth R. and Anderson, Herbert. Pages 50, 65. *All Our Losses, All Our Griefs,* Resources for Pastoral Care. Philadelphia: Westminster Press, 1983.
An exploration of the origins of grief, loss

throughout life, dynamics of grief, care for those who grieve, and the theology of grieving.

Nouwen, Henri J.M. Page 73. *Beyond the Mirror.* New York: Crossroad Publishing Co., 1990.
An interesting account of Nouwen's near death experience when he was struck by an automobile.

Oden, Marilyn Brown. Pages 91, 119. *Through the East Window.* Nashville: Upper Room Books, 1998.
Offers help in grieving during various kinds of loss including the death of a marriage and physical and mental impairment.

Overton, Patrick. Page 104. Overton is a poet and playwright, a nationally recognized community arts developer, and author of the *Faith Poem.* www.patrickoverton.com

Dr. Seuss. Page 42. *I Had Trouble in Getting to Solla Sollew.* New York: Random House, 1965.
One of dozens of delightfully imaginative stories written for children.

Tillich, Paul. Page 29. *The New Being.* New York: Charles Scribner's Sons, 1955.
A very helpful collection of sermons from this major twentieth century theologian.

Ziglar, Zig. Page 27. *Confessions of a Grieving Christian.* Nashville: Thomas Nelson Publishers, 1998.
The author, a nationally-known motivational speaker and writer, gives a personal account of his struggles in dealing with the death of his forty-six-year-old daughter.

Hymns, Poems, and Miscellaneous References

Page 106. *Book of Common Prayer, The.* New York: Seabury Press, 1979. p. 481.

Page 84. Chisholm, Thomas O. "Great Is Thy Faithfulness." ©Hope Publishing Co., 1951. UM Hymnal, p. 140.

Page 107. Dorsey, Thomas A. "Precious Lord, Take My Hand." ©Unichapel Music, Inc. UM Hymnal, p. 474.

Page 41. Gaither, Gloria and William J. "Because He Lives." ©William J. Gaither. 1971. UM Hymnal, p. 364.

Page 71. Herbert, George. Source unknown.

Page 105. Hine, Stuart K. "How Great Thou Art." ©Manna Music, Inc., 1981. UM Hymnal, p. 77.

Page 64. Matheson, George. "O Love That Wilt Not Let Me Go." UM Hymnal, p. 480.

Page 120. "Ministry With Persons Going Through Divorce." UM Book of Worship, p. 626.

Page 118. "Ministry With Persons in Coma or Unable to Communicate." UM Book of Worship, p. 629.